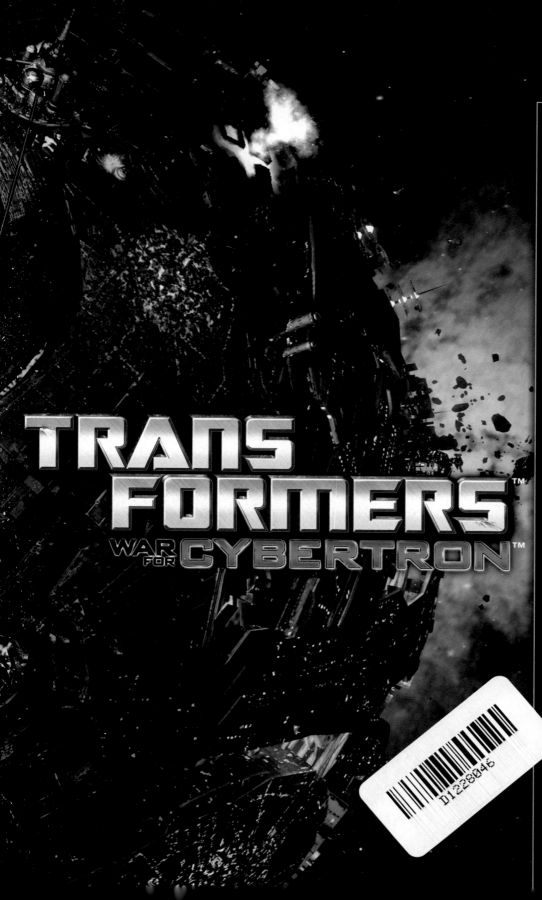

TRANS FORMERS™
WAR FOR CYBERTRON™

CHARACTERS. 2
  AUTOBOTS™ 2
    Optimus Prime 2
    Bumblebee 3
    Ratchet 3
    Sideswipe. 4
    Ironhide. 4
    Warpath 5
    Air Raid 5
    Jetfire 6
    Silverbolt. 6
    Arcee. 7
  DECEPTICONS™ 7
    Megatron 7
    Barricade 8
    Brawl. 8
    Starscream. 9
    Skywarp. 9
    Thundercracker 10
    Soundwave 10
    Breakdown. 11
    Slipstream. 11

ENEMIES 12

WEAPONS 15
  RANGED WEAPONS. 15
  MELEE WEAPONS 17
  GRENADES 17

GENERAL TIPS. 18

ABILITIES 19

POWER-UPS 19

MAIN STORY WALKTHROUGH 20
  01 DARK ENERGON 20
  02 FUEL OF WAR. 34
  03 IACON DESTROYED 50
  04 DEATH OF HOPE 66
  05 THE FINAL GUARDIAN 82
  06 DEFEND IACON 86
  07 KAON PRISON BREAK 102
  08 TO THE CORE 116
  09 AERIAL ASSAULT 128
  10 ONE SHALL STAND. 138

MULTIPLAYER. 144
  CLASSES 146
  MAPS 154
  CHALLENGES 158
  EXPERIENCE & LEVELING UP 168
  GENERAL MULTIPLAYER TIPS 171

ESCALATION 172
  MAPS 172
  GENERAL ESCALATION TIPS. 174

ACHIEVEMENTS/TROPHIES
& UNLOCKABLES 174

CHARACTERS

AUTOBOTS

The good-natured Autobots are the heroes of the Transformers universe. Originally, the Autobots were the worker class on Cybertron™. Sturdy, dependable, and built to last even through the toughest conditions, the Autobots adapted well in the war against their ageless enemy…the Decepticons.

OPTIMUS PRIME

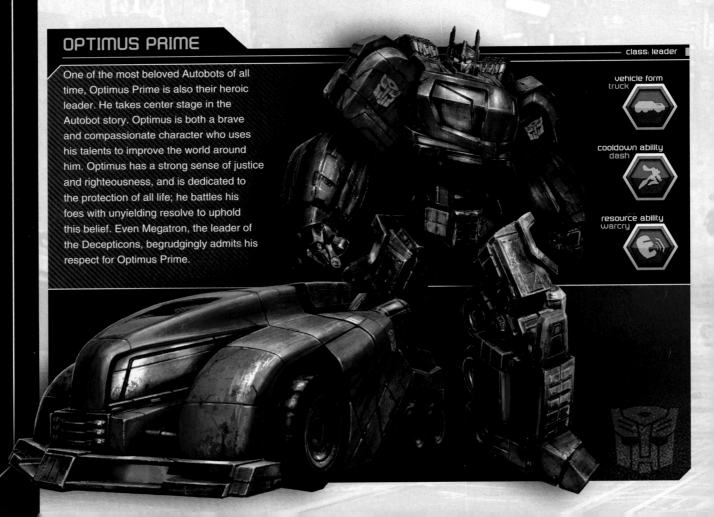

class: leader

One of the most beloved Autobots of all time, Optimus Prime is also their heroic leader. He takes center stage in the Autobot story. Optimus is both a brave and compassionate character who uses his talents to improve the world around him. Optimus has a strong sense of justice and righteousness, and is dedicated to the protection of all life; he battles his foes with unyielding resolve to uphold this belief. Even Megatron, the leader of the Decepticons, begrudgingly admits his respect for Optimus Prime.

vehicle form
truck

cooldown ability
dash

resource ability
warcry

BUMBLEBEE

class: scout

vehicle form
car

cooldown ability
dash

resource ability
shockwave

Being one of the smallest Autobots, Bumblebee excels in the art of espionage and reconnaissance. His small stature allows him to go places his comrades cannot. He deeply admires his larger, more physically capable teammates, and he does his best to emulate them. However, he does not realize that they deeply admire him for what he does. Bumblebee is a capable fighter fueled by his passionate devotion to the Autobot cause.

RATCHET

class: scientist

vehicle form
truck

cooldown ability
barrier

resource ability
spawn sentry

Ratchet is the Autobots' Chief Medical Officer. Although he's not a mighty warrior compared to the likes of Optimus Prime or Ironhide, Ratchet still often ends up in the center of battle. His dry wit helps him through it all, and he is always there after the fight to patch up his friends. As one would expect, he gives his wounded comrades a hard time for taking the hits that a Medical Officer somehow manages to avoid.

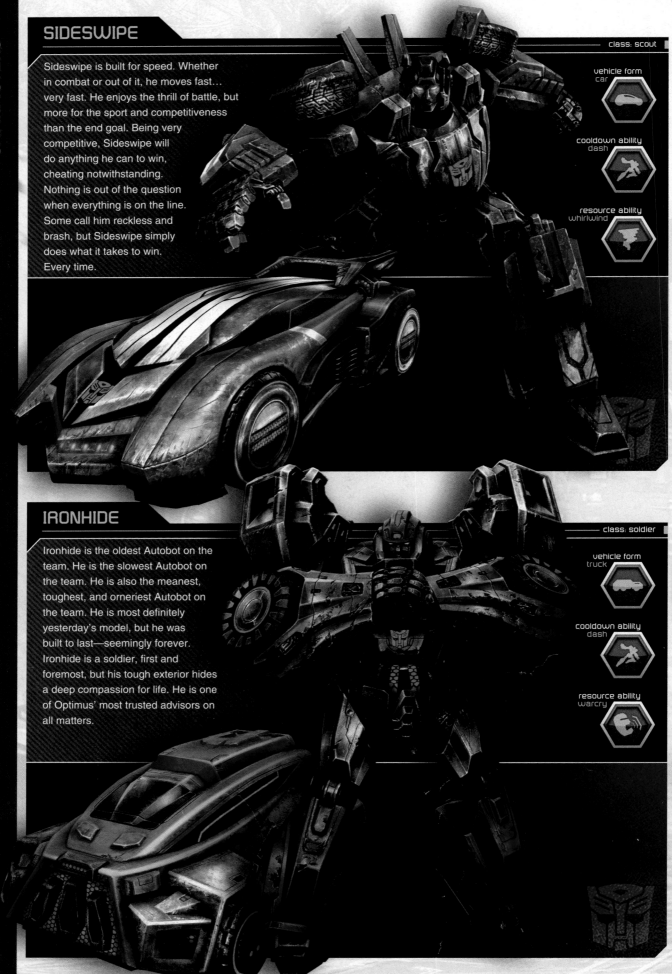

SIDESWIPE

class: scout

Sideswipe is built for speed. Whether in combat or out of it, he moves fast… very fast. He enjoys the thrill of battle, but more for the sport and competitiveness than the end goal. Being very competitive, Sideswipe will do anything he can to win, cheating notwithstanding. Nothing is out of the question when everything is on the line. Some call him reckless and brash, but Sideswipe simply does what it takes to win. Every time.

vehicle form
car

cooldown ability
dash

resource ability
whirlwind

IRONHIDE

class: soldier

Ironhide is the oldest Autobot on the team. He is the slowest Autobot on the team. He is also the meanest, toughest, and orneriest Autobot on the team. He is most definitely yesterday's model, but he was built to last—seemingly forever. Ironhide is a soldier, first and foremost, but his tough exterior hides a deep compassion for life. He is one of Optimus' most trusted advisors on all matters.

vehicle form
truck

cooldown ability
dash

resource ability
warcry

WARPATH

class: soldier

vehicle form tank

cooldown ability barrier

resource ability shockwave

Warpath is loud, confident, skilled, and devoted to his fellow Autobots. He is also partially deaf from his amazingly large cannon. His favorite pastime is showing his friends how he can split a hex nut a mile and a half away with a tank shell. Extremely well armored to go along with his extreme stubbornness and thick skull, Warpath always loves to bring the battle to the Decepticons.

AIR RAID

class: scout

vehicle form jet

cooldown ability cloak

resource ability whirlwind

Fearless and rash, Air Raid is always ready for a fight. He prefers diving head-first into a pack of Decepticons rather than shooting them from afar…because it's more fun. That is his only real goal in life: to have fun. This attitude seems to place Air Raid and his fellows in danger on a regular basis, but he always manages to get himself and his friends out of it.

JETFIRE

class: scientist

Jetfire is dedicated to the pursuit of science, and he believes technology will ultimately give the Autobots victory over the Decepticons. He became an Autobot after disagreeing with the methods used by the Decepticons and Starscream in particular. Jetfire keeps himself completely cutting edge and up-to-date, making him the fastest Autobot ever created.

vehicle form
jet

cooldown ability
hover

resource ability
spawn sentry

SILVERBOLT

class: soldier

Silverbolt is a grim and brave warrior, who often worries more about his teammates than himself. He is courageous, can fly at breakneck speeds, and truly believes in the Autobot cause. He would die in defense of his friends if ever given the opportunity.

vehicle form
jet

cooldown ability
barrier

resource ability
shockwave

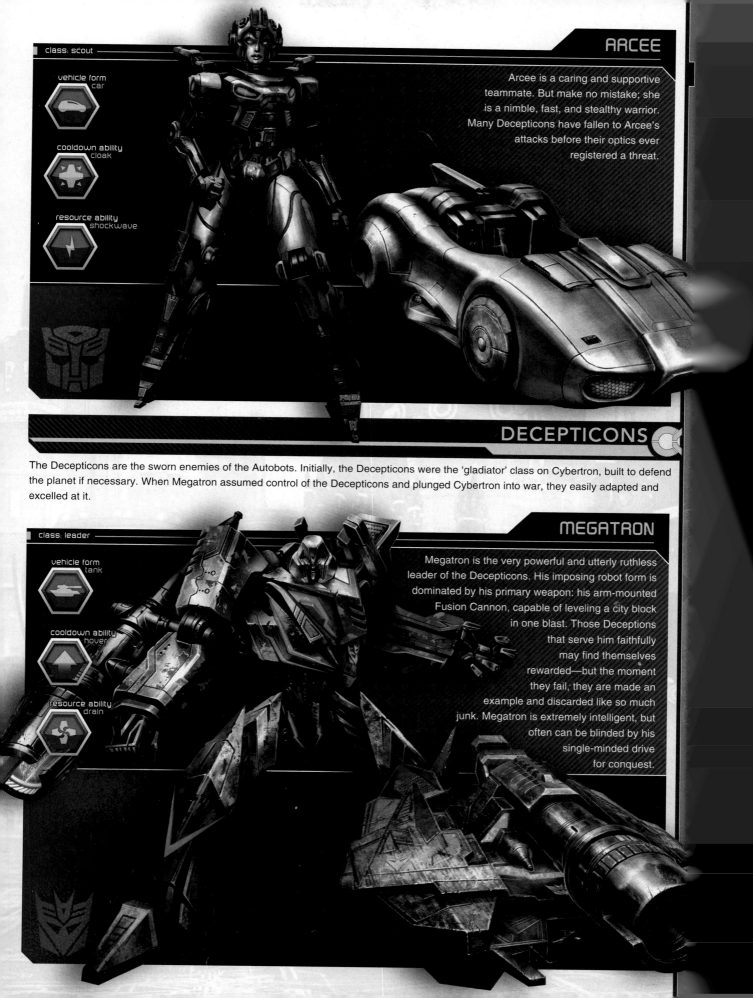

ARCEE

class: scout

vehicle form
car

cooldown ability
cloak

resource ability
shockwave

Arcee is a caring and supportive teammate. But make no mistake; she is a nimble, fast, and stealthy warrior. Many Decepticons have fallen to Arcee's attacks before their optics ever registered a threat.

DECEPTICONS

The Decepticons are the sworn enemies of the Autobots. Initially, the Decepticons were the 'gladiator' class on Cybertron, built to defend the planet if necessary. When Megatron assumed control of the Decepticons and plunged Cybertron into war, they easily adapted and excelled at it.

MEGATRON

class: leader

vehicle form
tank

cooldown ability
hover

resource ability
drain

Megatron is the very powerful and utterly ruthless leader of the Decepticons. His imposing robot form is dominated by his primary weapon: his arm-mounted Fusion Cannon, capable of leveling a city block in one blast. Those Deceptions that serve him faithfully may find themselves rewarded—but the moment they fail, they are made an example and discarded like so much junk. Megatron is extremely intelligent, but often can be blinded by his single-minded drive for conquest.

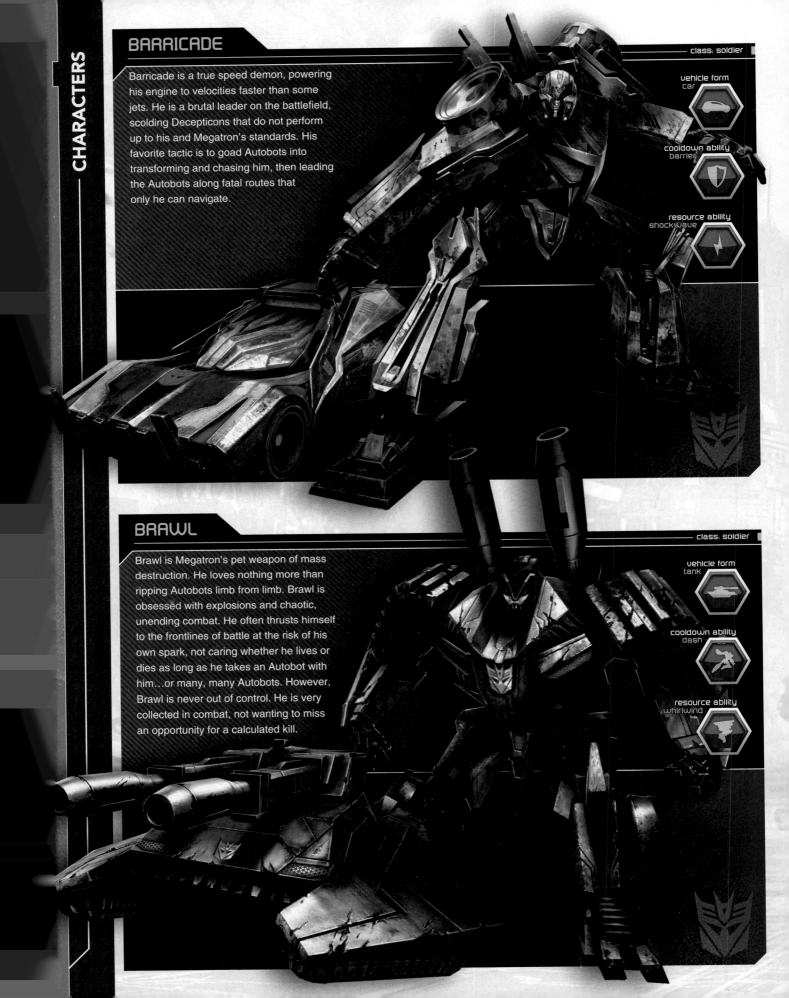

BARRICADE

class: soldier

Barricade is a true speed demon, powering his engine to velocities faster than some jets. He is a brutal leader on the battlefield, scolding Decepticons that do not perform up to his and Megatron's standards. His favorite tactic is to goad Autobots into transforming and chasing him, then leading the Autobots along fatal routes that only he can navigate.

vehicle form
car

cooldown ability
barrier

resource ability
shockwave

BRAWL

class: soldier

Brawl is Megatron's pet weapon of mass destruction. He loves nothing more than ripping Autobots limb from limb. Brawl is obsessed with explosions and chaotic, unending combat. He often thrusts himself to the frontlines of battle at the risk of his own spark, not caring whether he lives or dies as long as he takes an Autobot with him…or many, many Autobots. However, Brawl is never out of control. He is very collected in combat, not wanting to miss an opportunity for a calculated kill.

vehicle form
tank

cooldown ability
dash

resource ability
whirlwind

STARSCREAM

class: soldier

vehicle form
jet

cooldown ability
hover

resource ability
shockwave

Starscream is best known as the Decepticons' second-in-command. However, he makes no secret of his ambition to overthrow Megatron as Decepticon leader. He is more intelligent, ruthless, and cruel than the average Decepticon. But he is also unlikely to act directly on his ultimate ambition without an assurance of conditions favorable to his ascension. Starscream believes that both Optimus Prime and Megatron have lost sight of what is best for the Cybertronian race and simply pursue their own agendas. For the good of his species, he believes a new leader must emerge. He would be that leader.

SKYWARP

class: scout

vehicle form
jet

cooldown ability
cloak

resource ability
whirlwind

Skywarp isn't the most intelligent Transformer in the Decepticon force, so he must be guided continually and told what to do. Regardless, once set upon a path, Skywarp achieves his goal with quiet, ruthless efficiency.

THUNDERCRACKER

class: scientist

Serving alongside Starscream and Skywarp, Thundercracker is a part of the Decepticon Seekers' main force. Thundercracker despises Autobots and Decepticons that cannot take flight, and views himself as being superior to them. He reigns supreme in the air, having excellent skills in aerial combat and maneuvers. Thundercracker sometimes questions the Decepticon cause, but knowing Megatron's propensity for wrath and destruction, Thundercracker always remains quiet in his discontent.

vehicle form
jet

cooldown ability
dash

resource ability
spawn sentry

SOUNDWAVE

class: scientist

Soundwave is one of Megatron's most dependable troops. As such, he has positioned himself in Megatron's upper command structure. He operates as the Decepticon Communications Officer and answers only to Megatron. Many of the Decepticons see Soundwave as a backstabber who blackmails others to raise his esteem with Megatron. Soundwave sees and hears all.

vehicle form
truck

cooldown ability
barrier

resource ability
spawn sentry